AF480651

The Volcano, The Flame, and All I Became

EL HOFFMAN

To those who struggle to find a path forward: I've been there too.
Your path is ahead of you, even when you can't see it. You will
find your footing.
May your flame never go out.

A Note to Readers

As with all of my writing, this collection comes from a place of honesty. *The Volcano, The Flame, and All I Became* explores love, grief, and survival—and the person you become on the other side. At times, it depicts the raw pain of loss, heartbreak, and displacement. It is also one of the most unflinchingly honest things I've ever written.

I put a lot of emotion into *The Volcano, The Flame, and All I Became*, and I hope you'll love it as much as I do.

Content Warning

This book contains mild strong language, along with references to sexual assault, trauma, grief, mental health, and disability. While these subjects are explored through an artistic lens, reader discretion is advised.

"Saba"

They tried to tell me
that it wasn't you
who looked at me
that day,
but I know that it was you.

They looked like you,
dressed like you,
had the same belongings as you,
and pronounced things
the same way
that you do.

And I knew,
when you looked at me that day,
that you had forgotten who I was
and didn't care about me
anymore.

You would prefer
to keep with

the status quo,
rather than rocking the boat
and siding with me
over her.

Because at the end of the day,
it all comes down to her
and what she wants,
not me—
never me.

"Mirroring Your Dismay"

When you are in pain,
I feel it too—
exponentially so—
but I won't
split myself in half
to make you feel okay.

"Rollerskating"

I remember when we went rollerskating—
I fell so hard on my back
that when I yelled,
I bellowed.

You ignored me—
you didn't listen,
you didn't care,
you didn't help,
you weren't there.

And now, you wonder
why I don't talk to you
anymore.

"No One"

No one ever calls me,
except when they want to yell at me.
No one ever cares about me,
except if it will make them look better.
No one ever thinks of me,
unless I think of them first.
No one is ever there,
even when I'm there for them.
I'm better off on my own.

"I Joined"

I miss who I was
from before
I joined...

"When the Mask Slips"

The mask slips—
just a bit—
and now I am mocked,
by the people who should understand.

"So-Called 'Autism Moms'"

I don't know you personally,
but hand-flapping—
I don't think you've ever done.
The only autistic one
is my son,
and I want to keep him
under my thumb.

If you were autistic,
you would be ashamed—
you wouldn't call it by name.

The truth is—
I'm ashamed.
My son's behaviors—
I feel the same.
But I won't admit that,
so I cast blame.

You're a liar, you're a cheat,
I wouldn't see autism

if it were under my feet.

I tell myself
that Autism starts
at level two,
so I will not acknowledge you.

Autistic kids
never grow up, so adults like you
need to suck it up.

You're not disabled
because I said so—
don't tell me
when you can't get out of bed, though.

What's really happening
is that I don't want to lose control,
and level ones like you
make me fear I will lose my role.

Autistic you cannot be,
and unlike a chickadee,
I will not fly away.
The harassment
is here to stay.

"I Will Say it Again"

I want to call you,
but I tell myself that I will do it tomorrow.
And tomorrow, I will say it again.

"Eventually Decide"

I was worried
because I thought you'd eventually decide
I wasn't enough for you
or right for you
or exactly what you wanted—
and I was right.

"I Saw You Drive Past"

I saw you drive past—
at least,
I think that was you.
It's hard to tell
when all cars look the same
and high speeds mean you pass by
in a blink.

"Neurodivergent"

Being neurodivergent means that
people will hate you
no matter what you do.

"Enmeshment"

You think I'm part of you,
and I'm not.

"Emotionally Abusive Relationship"

When you turn normal boundaries into "control,"
basic care into "coercion,"
and asked-for guidance into "manipulation,"
it reflects poorly on you—
not me.

"Fourth of July"

You treated me as if
on the Fourth of July,
I said,
"Hey, let's get out of the country
for the day.
I hate fireworks."

And you said,
"Shush, hun.
I know we're in line
at the chicken place drive-thru,
but there's something I need to do,"
before buying
a truck bed of fireworks
and wondering why I left
when you lit them off.

"*Divorce*"

I never believed in divorce
until I saw how he treated you.

"Photos Not Taken"

This is a memorial
for the photos not taken
due to a low phone battery
or happenstance,
and those deleted
that shouldn't have been.

"Blueberry Muffin"

I was
a blueberry muffin,
and you crumbled me—
now I need
to frost myself
back together.

"Rose-Tinted Glasses"

I get sad when I think about the past.
Rose tinted glasses
and nostalgia
are painful.

"Here I Go"

Here I go again,
upset about things
that I thought
I had buried
down deep

"Ghost"

I am haunted
by a ghost from my past.

"I See Things"

I see things
a lot more clearly,
now that I have
stepped away.

"I Knew Immediately"

Have you ever met someone
and then immediately knew
that you're going to fall in love
with them?

"Hope for the Future"

Loving someone now or
having loved someone in the past
doesn't mean you can't love someone else
in the future.

"The Otorhinolaryngological"
PREVIOUSLY PUBLISHED BY POETS CHOICE

I met you
standing in front of
the otorhinolaryngological—
the ear, nose, and throat—
at the hospital.

You took both my hands and said,
"We've got to go."

I never looked back.

"A Text I Didn't Send"

Hey, I hope that you're doing okay—
I've had some time to think,
and I'd be open to catching up sometime
if you are.

"I Can't Drive"

Everyone seems to think that
when it suddenly becomes too cumbersome,
the driver's license and car keys appear in my hand,
and as soon as the rain stops,
I go back to not being able to drive.
Surely, I'm able to drive when it's raining,
surely I don't walk when it's raining.
No one walks in the rain, they say.
Except I can't drive on any day,
not just today—
so I walk away.

"Always On My Mind"

No matter where I go,
I can't get away from you.
You are in my head—
in my thoughts,
in everything I think of,
and in everything I do.

I can't date other people,
because I end up wanting you instead.
I can't distract myself,
because you're always in my head.
Late at night, I wake up,
thinking that you were still in my bed,
but I won't see you there again,
except in my head.

I don't know what to make of this,
because it's not as it seems,
I know that we aren't meant to be
outside of my dreams.

But someone told me recently
that they thought I was wrong
and that you like me too,
as if this were some kind of song.
But even though for your heart I long,
I know that you want any other but me.
Castaway, I am, forever to be.

Yet no matter the time,
you are always on my mind.

"Until the End"

What I actually want in a partner...
is you.

I look for you in everyone I meet, in everyone I talk to, and in
    everyone I pursue.
But no one is ever you,
except for you.

I joke with you and laugh with you
and want you to be happy,
and I always say I want you to find the one,
but when I think of who the one is
for me,
I always think of you.

For you, I think it is someone else,
but for me,
it is you.

And because of that, I am content to be alone
and watch you find someone who makes you happy,

because you are my rock,
and I measure everyone else against you.

We weren't perfect, no,
but you were—
and that's why I want you to be happy.
You deserve someone you would choose without hesitation,
and I know that isn't me.

Some days I say that I only love you as a friend,
but on other days I know that's just pretend.
Regardless of this trend,
I know that I want you in my life until the end.

"Big House"

I still remember
the first time I visited you—
you looked so small
all alone
in that big house.

"Forever Together, Together Forever"

· Spending a long time apart
made me realize how much
I want to spend forever together.

"Eternal Commitment"

I want you to commit
to me and only me
for time
and all eternity.

"Afraid of Rejection"

I am too afraid
to ask for what I want,
so I assume
the answer is no.

" *In Mine* "

I've written similar lines about beds to people i've never shared
    them with,
but I'll always remember what it felt like
to have you in mine.

"Denial"

As much as I hate the feeling,
I hope that you
are living in denial too.

"Recently, I Read"

I read something recently
that said
you should think with your heart
and not your head,
because making decisions with your head
doesn't appease your heart,
but making decisions without your head
can hurt your heart too,
so there's really no winning.

"Tell Me"

I can't expect clarity
if I only express indirectly,
but I need people
to tell me what they want
or I will never assume correct correctly.

"Red String"

If someone really loves me,
I won't have to have a bulletin board
with random quotes
tied with red string
to convince myself they do.

"Are You Real?"

Am I holding something real,
or a mirage?

"Prevent That"

Humans have free will,
and I won't prevent that.

I just wish
you would choose me.

"*The Disco*"

I flew to the disco
for you,
Sir.

How dare you.

"Choosing You"

I might love
someone else
too,
but I am choosing
you.

"Options"

I don't care if I have
a million other options
or zero,
I would choose you every time.

"Love/Hate"

I hate that
I love you.

"Wasn't Good"

I know that he wasn't good for me,
but I still miss him.

"Screwing Me Over"

Screwing me over
when I'm overstimulated
is not
cool
or cute
or okay.

It's not funny
or fair
if it puts me in despair.

"Haven't a Clue"

Some people aren't for you,
yet they haven't a clue.

"Doormat"

I'm glad that
now, at least,
I have a doormat,
but I'm glad I didn't become one.

"Second Best"

I don't want
to be
treated as if
I'm second best.

"Salt Lake City"

The trains announcing "Trolley,"
the streets with sidewalks,
the sugar cookies,
and the conformity.

I will always love
Salt Lake City.

"Too Soon"

Not saying thank you
doesn't mean you're not grateful.

"Story of My Life"

That didn't come out how I thought it would:
a memoir

"Up the Coast"

It only took
dragging my suitcases
up an entire coast
to move on
from you.

"Psychic or Stubborn?"

Am I a psychic,
or am I just stubborn?

"I Won't Bother"

If you can't even spell your criticism correctly,
why would I bother listening to it?
Why would I let it affect me,
when you can't spell it properly?

"Ignoring"

I don't know why everyone is ignoring me,
but I know that I don't deserve it.

"*Suitcases*"

My suitcases get lighter,
the pain does not.

"Anxiety"

Anxiety:
tomorrow's problems, today.

"I'll Always Care"

But when your area makes headlines,
I always check to make sure you weren't involved.
I'll always care,
even if I don't remind you of that.

"Headache"

Sometimes
a headache
is just
a headache.

"I Can't Stop"

No matter what I do,
I cant stop going back to you.

"Comic Relief"

I'm pretty good at caricatures,
I used to draw comics.

"Choked"

I don't want to be unequally yoked
But I'd rather be unequally yoked
than unwantedly choked.

"Don't"

If someone tells you,
with a straight face,
not to contact them again,
don't.

"Never Works"

Trying to force yourself
to be something you're not
never works.

"Distance Yourself"

Distance yourself
from those
who make everything
about them.

"*Lavender Nights*"

I guess that
it wasn't right
for us to share our lavender nights.

"Upsetting"

I need to move past
my fear of upsetting people.

"Two Sides, Same Coin"

You were both great
and abusive,
and that dynamic
makes it hard
to move on
from you.

"Caring"

I'm done caring about people
who don't care about me.

"Playing House"

I wanted a spouse,
but you were just playing house.

"Explaining Reality"

I feel like I'm trying to explain
human reality
to a chimpanzee
and they kind of
maybe
sort of
almost
get it
but not completely
because they're a f***ing monkey.

"I Need to Address It"

I know that you hate
when I put you under the spotlight,
but something came up
and I need to address it.

"Be Alone"

And again,
I realize
that I am meant to be alone.

"Unloved"

I'm still in love with someone
who will never love me
again.

"Always You"

I change my mind
all the time
about everything
but all I know for certain
is that
I always want
what I can't have
(you).

"Agree to Disagree"

Not being able
to agree to disagree
is on you
not me

"Clown, Not Down"

It's crazy
when you invite someone over,
and they don't leave.
You didn't ask them to stay the night.

You say you're going to bed.
They say they'll be quiet, before laying down.
Am I the clown?
Well, I'm certainly not down.

"The Lies We Tell"

I am not that,
but I can be if you want me to be.
(Please say no.)

"*Strange*"

I don't know what was wrong with me—
I felt really strange
and I don't want to repeat that.

"Eleven"

On a scale from one
to ten,
my obviousness
is an eleven.

"*Cannot Silence*"

The thing is,
you want to silence me—
which just makes me
more unabashedly myself.

"Mr. I'm a Genius"

I make things up
as if I'm speaking with the divine,
and *oh* that lady is fine!

Did you know that my IQ is a million?
I'm an elitist, but that's okay—
I know that I'm better any time of day.

I bow down to Machiavelli,
but a narcissist I cannot be.
I'm smarter than the doctors,
they cannot trounce me.

Now please get down on one knee.

"Sportsball"

All sportsball
is the same
to me.

"Honesty is the Best Policy"

I will not lie
to appease other people.

"Pedestrian Life"

You think you know the world better,
because you sit in your car.
But I know the world better,
because I navigate transit
here and far.

The pedestrian life I live,
twelve or more miles I walk.
Trains and buses I ride.
I know the world intimately,
not the parking lots.
Not heated seats.
Not air conditioning
and speakers.

The roads,
the intersections,
the sidewalks,
the paths,
the transit—
I know them all.

You have a car,
you travel far.
I travel here,
I don't live in fear.
The streets are safe,
but if they weren't,
it wouldn't change.
I do as I please,
and my hair blows in the breeze.
My life is less stressful,
far more carefree.

Rain, snow, shine, just not ice.
I don't revolve my life
around a box on wheels.
Wouldn't that be nice?
No, I can't drive—
I prefer the pedestrian life.

The train stops
are said aloud.
I can't get lost,
but if I do,
I'll find the route.
Streets are near,
streets are far,
transit is better
than any car.

You are stuck in your car—
but wherever I go,
the world is mine to know.

"In My Dreams"

In my dreams, I imagine storming in the office
and kicking down the door,
telling you to get your shit together.
But in reality, I know to be civil,
so I do anything but.

"Omission"

Lying by omission
is still lying.

"Accountability"

There's a difference
between taking accountability
and telling me what you think
I want to hear.

"*Little City*"

I love
my little city.

"Marry"

You think that I
just want to
marry anyone,
but no,
I want the right one.
Not just anyone.

"Morality"

I refuse to submit
to an authority
who wants to control
my choices—
and my morality.

I deserve
to make my own choices
about my own life
and my own body
(my actual body).

I will not feel ashamed
when doing nothing wrong.
I will not cower
under authority I didn't ask for

I will be myself
and if that's a problem,
you can kindly leave.

"Want/Need"

A want
is not a need.

"*Mother*"

I do not want
to mother
my boyfriend.

"Stop Speaking"

Stop speaking
on
what you don't know.

"*Logic Away*"

You can't logic away
anxiety

"Mentally"

I understand what you are saying logically,
but that doesn't change how I feel mentally.

"If Not Travel?"

Traveling is weird
because I'm in the future,
but my present is the future
and the future is my present
and you're in the past
and I need to travel back to the past,
but then it will be my present.
What is time, if not travel?

"I Said Goodbye"

Looking back,
Mr. Doodyhead,
I realize why you never loved me—
and it's that
you never loved yourself,
and you took that out on me.
But I love myself,
and I deserve better—
that's why
I said goodbye.

"Tolerate"

I do not
tolerate disrespect.

"Opens Your Mind"

Travel
opens your mind
to a wide range of new ideas—
but you wanted to keep me small.

"Coming Back"

I have accepted
that you
are not coming back

"*Husband*"

I realized
that we are in
completely different
stages of life.

You want a mother,
and I want a husband.

"*Moldy*"

I am frustrated,
because every time
I look at moving
elsewhere,
I get excited,
and then
I realize
how moldy it is
there,
so I am unable to go.

"Frustrating"

It's frustrating,
because if someone else has a migraine,
they get the day off.
If I have a migraine, it's just another day.

"Square"

I've always heard
not to jam
a square peg
into a round hole.

I'm a square peg,
and I don't want someone round.

"Ostrich"

The answers are right in front of you,
yet you bury your head in the sand.

"The Weather"

The sky was supposed to be clear today,
but the thing about weather
is that you never know what to expect.

"Legal"

I don't think some people understand this,
but "legal" doesn't mean
"good."

"Convenient"

You said
that you wanted to be with someone like you,
that way, she would understand—
but you only wanted
to understand me
when it was convenient.

"Throw"

Sometimes
you just have to
throw the whole man away.

"Macadamias"

And yes,
this is all about
the macadamias.

"Whims"

If they ignore your needs
for their whims,
they are not meant for you.

"How?"

How could you
do that to me?

"Cared"

If you cared about me,
you wouldn't do that to me.

"No Interest"

I have no interest
in speaking to people
who ignore me.

"Talk to You"

Why would I want to talk to you
if you can't hear me
or understand me?

"*Unwell*"

People who don't check on you
when they know you're unwell
don't care.
There's no use denying it.

"Smiling"

Smiling
doesn't mean
I'm happy.

"Wide Brush"

I hate
painting with a wide brush.
Stereotypes
are not always accurate.

"Safety Hazard, M.D."

You asked me to trust you.
So I fell back,
intending to land in your arms.
But you weren't there,
and you let me fall—
alone.

Then you came back
and said you would take care of me.
Just to abandon me yet again,
when I needed you most.

Why weren't you there for me,
Safety Hazard, M.D.?

"No Contact Until Then"

If you reach out to me again,
I need to know how it will benefit me—
and if you will stay with me until the end,
so no contact until then.

"Meaningless"

Your word is meaningless
when you don't ever follow through—
I can't trust you.

"White Cars II"

I think that it will take a while
for me to stop looking at
white cars
expecting to see you.

"A Painting"

When I think of us,
I think of a painting where two people are both touching a
    wall,
wondering if the other person is thinking of them.
The person on the left is turned towards the right
and the person on the right is turned towards the left.
They're both touching a wall—
not the same wall, but the same in spirit,
turned towards each other, even when they didn't know it.
They're both black and white outlines with black and white
    backgrounds,
opposite color schemes to each other,
but they're both touching the wall thinking and longing
    about if the other person is thinking of them.
They're both doing it at the same time.
This painting is powerful
and moving
and beautiful—
if only it existed.

"Took You For Granted"

I wish I could say that I took you for granted,
that I regret acting the way that I did,
and that I should've tried to not let my emotions control me
    in the way that they did—
but you left me,
and maybe it was for the best.

"Crazy One"

At least I know
that I wasn't the crazy one.

"Ended"

I feel like I was grieving the relationship
before it even ended.

"I Still Love You"

I remember meeting you.
I didn't know who you were, but I wanted to talk to you
    more.
And then we were able to talk more, I wanted to get to
    know you.
I needed to know your name, and I found it.
So I reached out, but it didn't work.
And then you reached out, it was mutual.
We messaged a bit, and then you asked me out.
And we hit it off.
And we fell in love.
And I miss that.
And I wish that we could get back to that.
I still love you.

"Very Sad"

It's sad,
very sad.

"May Never Be"

I feel a rush of excitement and then disappointment and
    sadness
every time my watch vibrates
with a text.

It's not you—
it's never you.
And may never be you
again.

Every time I see a funny video
I think you may have liked,
I cry a little
then.

Every time I smell you on my sheets,
I'm reminded of home
and cry again.

When I think of the looks I had seen
on your face

I feel like nothing will ever replace
what I had with you—
and the way you made me feel.

No matter how many times I give the spiel
of what we went through,
I can't seem to move past you.

Sometimes I feel like I didn't have a clue
what I was losing
when I lost you.

You were my everything.
Not just my partner,
but my friend and compadre and companion and jokester.
Those little moments,
I don't think I'll ever get over.

I think that maybe—
in the future—
we could make things work,
but I hate to get my hopes up
just for them to go down
again.

In the night I roll over,
expecting to see you asleep.
But you're never there,
and for that,
I grieve.

You were something special
and the grass isn't greener.
I wish I would've seen that
before things got clearer

and the end came nearer.

It's you—
always you.
And I miss you—
always you.
I love you—
always you.

"Get Better"

I was trying to get better so that I could be there for you
the way you were for me—
until you left me.

"Coat"

I know I wasn't perfect,
but I tried my hardest.
I tried to be there for you,
and I wanted to buy you a coat
to keep you warm.
I wanted to be there for you
when the world was dark—
and when things were falling apart.

"Two Things Are True"

I miss you,
but you hurt me,
but I miss you.

"*Your Sanity*"

Sometimes when you think you lost someone,
you actually gained your sanity.

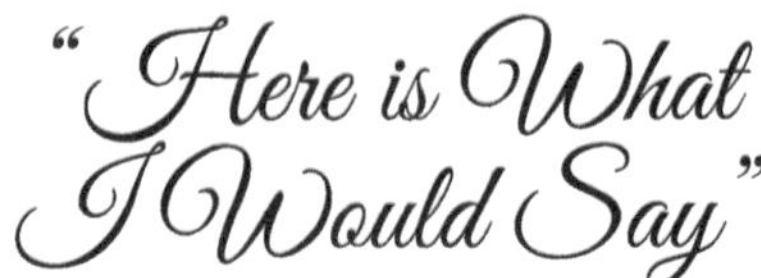

Here is what I would say to you,
if I could say anything at all:

I miss the way that you would laugh when I would say some-
    thing funny
and the way you understood my sense of humor.

I miss the way that you would make me laugh, because it's not
    always the easiest thing to do.

I miss the inside jokes that we had and the ways that we would
    goof around.

I miss when we would care for each other, the way that no one
    else could—
or would.

I miss when I would steal your hat and make funny faces, and
    flip your glasses upside down.

I miss that day that I stole your tie, just to goof around.

I miss hearing about your day and the things that made you
    smile,
even if after a while,
I didn't have the energy to hear the negative parts.

I miss your little bit with the walk sign
that you would always do—
I wonder if you still do that, too.

I know that we weren't a good fit,
for numerous reasons why.
But you know that I did everything I could to try.
Even when I feel my brain fry,
I still miss you,
even when I can't point my finger on why.

If nothing else,
I wanted you to be my friend—
here with me until the end.

But you didn't want that,
and I wasn't going to plead—
because I need
someone who will never think
to leave.

I hope that
you will never doubt my care
even if someone says or assumes contraire—
I always wanted
to be there.

I find myself
with more energy now,
but I would trade that

for the beginning, how.

A part of me knows this is for the best,
but self-inquiry tells me that I can't reason
the rest.
Opposite action tells me to face my fears,
yet I don't trust myself
to go near;
unless the path forward is clear—
it isn't worth the risk.

If someone from my past regrets their actions,
they should be the one to give me that reaction—
not me, never me.

I need to live my life—
an apology isn't necessarily rife.
But if it is,
I'll consider it then—
I just won't think
as to when.

I deserve the best,
as do you,
as does everyone,
even those
who don't have a clue.

And as for you,
sending my best—
but for now, I will pause to rest.
Until it is rife,
I will not sacrifice.

"Get Sad"

When I get sad,
I wonder if you are too.
I miss you.

"All People Do"

I just have a hard time believing you
when all people do
is leave.

"Regret"

I thought that you regretted your actions,
so why did you repeat them?

"In My Life"

I miss you,
but that doesn't mean I can handle having you
in my life.

"Call Out to Sea"

All I want is you.
You're the moor to my boat,
the wind in my sails.
No matter what life entails,
I know that I'll always love you.

You're my call out to sea,
all I want or need,
the air that I breathe.

You're the sunlight on the water,
the scent in the air,
the deck beneath my feet,
the waves the tide pulls in,
and the love in my heart—
I never want to be apart.

When there's stillness on the water,
my thoughts drift to you.
When I dream at night,

it's always of you.
No matter what storms I may face,
I know that nothing could replace
what I feel for you—
always you.

"Okay Every Day"

I think about you every day,
but I just hope that you're okay.

"Anyway"

You said
that when it got sunny,
things would be better
for me—
and for us.

Then on the first sunny day,
you left me anyway.

"Olive Branch"

I extended an olive branch
just for you
to bite down and cranch—
who eats an olive branch?

"*A Love Letter to Bratislava*"

I love the UFOs—
Most SNP and UFO Sancho,
the views from Eurovea Tower,
the vegan halusky.

You are Roswell, but better.
Tel Aviv is the only one
who can surpass you—
all of me
loves you.

"Sleep Through Turbulence"

I don't understand
how some people can
sleep through turbulence.

"Repeating"

You can say that you believe that all day long,
but I know that you're just repeating it
out of habit.

"Former Member"

When everyone keeps telling you
you're making a good decision,
it's hard to sort out the noise
from the truth.

"My Constitution"

If you choose an institution
over me,
you will never again see
my constitution.

"*Lying to Myself*"

I try not
to lie
to other people,
yet I don't seem
to mind
lying to myself.

"More Than Life Itself"

You can
love someone
more than
life itself,
and still know
that dating them
would destroy you.

"Evil"

You can be well intentioned
and still be evil.

"The Grass That Grew"

The grass that grew,
but never knew.

"As Important"

I received a reminder
that I am not as important to people
as they are
to me.

"Petty Rejection"

I would rather hand you
a petty rejection
than deal with
your constant deflection.

"That Song"

I can't listen to that song
without thinking of you
and how we danced together
in that low lighting.

"Our Old Pictures"

I looked at our old pictures
and it hit me
how stupid I have been.

"Tail Lights"

I cried
while I watched you
walk to your car
and drive away

I stayed there crying
until your tail lights
were out of sight

"Oblivious"

You are so oblivious,
but I love you for it—
even if it drives me crazy.

"A Song"

I sent you a song
because it made me think of you—
yearning, missing, wanting to kiss you
and escape with you.
Wanting you to notice me and want me too.

And you said that you like the song.
Not that you like me,
not that you miss me,
not that you want me—
that you like the *song*.

The song was irrelevant—
it was about the lyrics and vibe and emotion.
And you liked the song—
not me.

" *Fresh Air* "

I can't get a fresh breath of air
because you are always there.

"Two Soulmates"

Sometimes I wonder
if we have two soulmates,
one of which
we can't have.

"Lie in It"

I really regret last night,
but I told myself I made my bed
and I have to lie in it.

"Really Regret It Now"

You had dressed up for me
for the first time—
you looked so fucking nice.
We went to one of my favorite restaurants—
you paid for our dinner.
You even winked at me.

I wanted it to be such a beautiful night.
I wanted to have fun with you.
I wanted to dance and twirl around—
but because of what happened,
I just didn't see a path forward—
but I really regret it now.

"Proposed"

I still remember
when you had proposed,
and I had said yes—
not because I wanted to,
but I felt like I had no other option.

I'll forever be grateful
that you had "forgotten"
that you had asked
the
very
next day.

"Basic Skills"

No,
I don't want to
show you
how to do
basic skills—
I had to learn on my own,
so you can too—
or not at all.

"Looking Back"

Looking back,
why did I ever get involved with you?

"*Lately*"

Lately, I've been rejecting
what other people want for me.
I feel better.
Truly.

"Betray My Trust"

How could you
betray my trust
and then wonder
why I don't want
to talk to you?

"One-Sided"

It doesn't matter what I want
when everything with you is so one-sided—
you say one thing
and do another.

"You Deserve Better"

If you're reading this,
you are probably not the problem—
and you deserve better.

"*Aleph*"

It isn't all about you,
even though you think it is.
I will decide my path now—
you don't get to dictate my life
going forward.

I've spent too long
cowering under you,
but you don't get to decide
what I choose to do.

I'm done being controlled
and judged
and mocked
by you,
Aleph.

What Some People Expected Me to Write

I'm not writing from the vantage point of a suburban mom with a minivan and a Costco membership. I never said I was.

I'm child-free, I can't drive, and I don't like Costco.

I don't write from the perspective of someone who drives everywhere and has kids—because I don't drive, and I don't have kids.

I write from the perspective of someone who walks, takes trains, and thinks too much.

That's not a flaw. That's a point of view.

But apparently, some people expected something different.

POV ≠ universal experience. Not every book is for every reader—and that's fine.

So here is that section.

You don't have to relate to me.

You just have to be willing to listen.

"Traffic"

Traffic is bad,
and I hate my life.

"Neighbors"

Neighbors are good,
neighbors are bad.
But unfortunately—
they were all that I had.

"Paper Towels"

I like paper towels,
paper towels are good.

Acknowledgments

I would like to thank Sam Bolano for his work as my illustrator. I would also like to thank my readers for allowing my vision to take root in your minds.

The Volcano, The Flame, and All I Became was written during a pivotal part of my life—while taking time off work, traveling, undergoing considerable stress, and choosing to convert to Judaism. You may see those themes reflected in the pages, but art is subjective.

"The Otorhinolaryngological" was first published by Poets Choice. All rights to the poem remain with me, but they receive first publication credit.

The volcano in question is Vesuvius—number one on my bucket list for a reason. Hiking it was the most peaceful experience of my life: above Naples, surrounded by fog, steam rising from the crater, no cell service. There is something humbling about standing on a mountain that has taken so many lives and could again at any moment. Truly unmatched.

I hope you enjoyed *The Volcano, The Flame, and All I Became*. If you did, please consider leaving a review on Amazon and/or Goodreads, and if you'd like to read further, my first and second collections, *The Mirror, The Mask, and All I Ask* and *The Moon, The Tide, and All I Tried*, are also available.

About the Author

El Hoffman (born February 8, 2000) is an author, poet, and data expert. A lifelong writer, she debuted with the literary fantasy novella *The Ever-Dark*. The novelette *The Scarlet-Dawn* serves as its direct sequel. El is also the author of the contemporary romance novelette *No Other Reason* and three poetry collections: *The Mirror, The Mask, and All I Ask*; *The Moon, The Tide, and All I Tried*; and *The Volcano, The Flame, and All I Became*. Her work has also been featured in multiple anthologies.

Outside of fiction, El has built a career implementing HubSpot for businesses and earned her Master of Science in Data Analytics from Eastern University in 2024.

When she's not writing or working, she enjoys reading ebooks, taking long walks, and hula hooping. She's also passionate about video games, cooking, exploring new restaurants, and traveling.

instagram.com/elhoffmanauthor

tiktok.com/@elhoffmanauthor

amazon.com/author/elhoffman

bookbub.com/authors/el-hoffman

threads.com/@elhoffmanauthor

youtube.com/@elhoffmanauthor